FIRST
PEOPLES
of NORTH
AMERICA

THE PEOPLE AND CULTURE OF THE
INUIT

RAYMOND BIAL

Cavendish
Square

New York

Published in 2016 by Cavendish Square Publishing, LLC
243 5th Avenue, Suite 136, New York, NY 10016

Copyright © 2016 by Cavendish Square Publishing, LLC

First Edition

Library of Congress Cataloging-in-Publication Data

Bial, Raymond.
The people and culture of the Inuit / Raymond Bial.
pages cm. — (First peoples of North America)
Includes bibliographical references and index.
ISBN 978-1-5026-1006-5 (hardcover) ISBN 978-1-5026-1007-2 (ebook)
1. Inuit—Juvenile literature. 2. Eskimos—Juvenile literature. I. Title.
E99.E7B49 2015
305.897'12—dc23

2015023768

Editorial Director: David McNamara
Editor: Kristen Susienka
Copy Editor: Nathan Heidelberger
Art Director: Jeffrey Talbot
Designer: Amy Greenan
Senior Production Manager: Jennifer Ryder-Talbot
Production Editor: Renni Johnson
Photo Research: J8 Media

ACKNOWLEDGMENTS

The People and Culture of the Inuit could not have been written without the kind help of many people and organizations that have devoted themselves to preserving the traditions of the Inuit.

   I would like to acknowledge Cavendish Square Publishing for publishing the manuscript. As always, I offer my deepest thanks for my wife, Linda, and my children, Anna, Sarah, and Luke, for their wonderful inspiration.

CONTENTS

An Inuit woman wears
a traditional costume.

AUTHOR'S NOTE

At the dawn of the twentieth century, Native Americans were thought to be a vanishing race. However, despite four hundred years of warfare, deprivation, and disease, Native Americans have persevered. Countless thousands have lost their lives, but, over the course of this century and the last the populations of Native tribes have grown tremendously. Even as America's First People struggle to adapt to modern Western life, they have also kept the flame of their traditions alive—the languages, religions, stories, and the everyday ways of life. An exhilarating renaissance in Native American culture is now sweeping the continent from coast to coast.

The First Peoples of North America books depict the social and cultural life of the major nations, from the early history of Native peoples in North America to their present-day struggles for survival and dignity. Historical and contemporary photographs of traditional subjects, as well as period illustrations, are blended throughout each book so that readers may gain a sense of family life in a tipi, a hogan, or a longhouse.

No single book can comprehensively portray the intricate and varied lifeways of an entire tribe, or nation. I only hope that young people will come away with a deeper appreciation for the rich tapestry of Native American culture—both then and now—and a keen desire to learn more about these first Americans.

An Inuit mother and child, circa 1927

CHAPTER ONE

There are few people in America who can say that their forebears were here 10,000 years ago."

—William L. Hensley, Inupiat elder

A CULTURE BEGINS

Native Americans have lived in North America for many thousands of years. At first, they came into the continent by way of a land bridge across the **Bering Strait**. Some arrived in groups that stayed together and others in groups that went their separate ways over time. Before long, pockets of Native communities were spread throughout the entire continent.

This map shows the regions where Inuit live today.

By the time the first Europeans arrived, these Native men, women, and children had created unique communities with their own traditions, beliefs, and customs. One of these groups was the Inuit (IN-oo-it), a group that stayed together for much of its history and continues to live life in the northernmost reaches of the world.

Origins of the Inuit

Once known as Eskimos, the Inuit have long inhabited parts of northern Asia and North America. Here, a vast land of ice and snow stretches from Siberia across

Alaska to eastern Canada and Greenland. It is a remote area, seemingly at the top of the world. In this region, the sun follows an unusual seasonal cycle, glowing day and night through the brief months of summer. Through the long winters, the sun sets in mid-November and does not reappear until mid-January.

For generations the Inuit have told stories to help them through the light-filled days and the long stretch of seemingly endless nights. Here is a version of one such tale told by Apagkaq, a Mackenzie River Inuit, about the raven and how people came to live in this harsh and challenging environment:

He was quite alone on Earth, squatting in the darkness. Suddenly he became conscious and discovered himself, but he had no idea where he was, nor did he know how he had gotten there, but he breathed, and there was life in him. He lived!

But who was he? A being—something living. Anything beyond that he could not comprehend. All about him was darkness, and he could see nothing.

Then he groped about with his hands. Wherever he touched, his fingers brushed over clay. The earth was lifeless clay, as was everything else about him.

He let his fingers glide over himself. He knew nothing of how he looked, but he found his face and felt that he had a nose, eyes and mouth, arms and legs, and limbs. He was a human being—a man!

He felt his forehead and found a hard little bump. What was that for?

He began to reflect. He understood that he was a separate being. He started to crawl across the clay, slowly and cautiously. He wanted to find out where he was. Yet suddenly his hands felt only empty space—an abyss— and he dared not go on.

He squatted and wondered how he might discover what the great black darkness held. He broke off a piece of clay and threw it into the abyss. He listened for the clay to reach the bottom, but no sound came back to him.

He moved away from the abyss and found a hard object on the ground. He pushed it into the clay. Why he did so he did not know; he simply did it. Then he sat still again, lost in thought and wondering what was in the darkness.

Suddenly a sound startled him. He heard a flutter in the air, and a small, light thing settled on his hand. With his other hand he touched this mysterious visitor and found that it had a bill, warm soft feathers all over its body, and small naked feet.

It was a little sparrow. All at once he understood that it had been there all along, flying over him and hopping about him in the darkness. He had simply not noticed the sparrow until it landed on his hand.

The man liked the company of the little bird. He felt bolder and crawled over the ground till he came to the object he had stuck into the clay. Then he discovered that it had taken root. A tree grew out of the ground, and soft grass had sprouted on the clay!

He crawled to the tree. Other trees had grown around it, one beside another. They had become a forest. Small plants formed a lush carpet on the forest floor, and he passed his hand over them. He felt their shape and smelled their fragrance, but still he could see nothing.

The man wanted to know more about this strange place, so he crept along with the little sparrow fluttering above his head. He could not see it, but he heard the sound of its wings. He also felt the bird when it settled on his head or hopped onto his hand. The man crawled because he dared not walk blindly through the darkness.

He wanted to know what was in the abyss and asked the sparrow to fly down and explore it. The little bird flew away. It was gone so long that the man thought the sparrow would never return. Finally, the sparrow returned and landed on his head holding a fresh shoot in its bill.

The fresh shoot made the man want to explore the depths of the abyss himself. He asked the sparrow to perch on his knee so he could examine its body to learn how it could fly on its small wings. Groping his way through the forest, the man broke off branches and attached them to his shoulders. As he flapped the branches, they became real wings. Feathers sprouted on his body and the lump on his forehead grew into a bill. Suddenly, he realized that he could fly like the little sparrow.

It was still dark, and he could see nothing. He asked the sparrow to fly in front of him so that he could hear the beating of its wings. As the man left the ground, he cried, "Kowk-kowk." He had turned into a big black bird, and he called himself a raven.

The raven named the place they had left the sky. It was a long way from the sky to the land of the abyss. The raven struggled to keep himself in the air, but he and the sparrow finally arrived at the land of the abyss. The raven planted the land of the abyss in the same manner as he had planted in the sky. Soon there was forest everywhere, and herbs and flowers grew among the trees. This new land the raven called the world.

Then the raven created people. He shaped them of clay. So there might be food for them, he created the animals of the land, air, and sea. He told the people of the world that these animals would sustain them.

In those first days of the world, nothing could be seen. The people had to feel or listen to find their way. The people heard caribou bulls calling in deep throaty tones, wolves howling, bears growling, foxes calling, "kak-kak-kak." From the sea they could hear the snorting of seals, the bellowing of walruses, and the calling of whales, "Puh-puh-puh!" They heard birds screaming and singing. They heard the sighing of the wind in the forests, the rustling and whispering of the leaves, and the crash of the breakers on the shore.

The people were surrounded by life and sound, but still they could see nothing. Everywhere they groped in the darkness. It was hard to catch animals for food, so the raven called the little sparrow and said, "You were there before I found myself sitting on the ground. Fly out into the world and find something to give us light so we may see one another, the land where we live, and the animals that feed us."

The sparrow flew away into the darkness. The little bird was gone so long that the raven thought it would never come back. Because there was no light, there was no day and night. There was also no time, so the raven had no idea how long the sparrow had been gone, but one day he heard the beat of its wings and felt it perch on his hand. In its bill were two pieces of mica wrapped in leaves. One piece was light, and the other was dark.

The raven broke off a small piece of the light mica and threw it into the air. At once a strong light flooded the world and dazzled all its inhabitants. For the first time the people could look out over the land on which they lived. They saw the forests, the animals on the ground and in the sea, and the birds in the air. They delighted in all the beauty around them.

However, the light was too strong. It dazzled them. So the raven broke off a piece of the dark mica and threw it into the air. At once the light grew dim. People could see without their eyes hurting, and eventually night came and gave them the rest they needed.

The people now needed shelter from wind and storms, so the raven taught them to build houses. The raven showed them how to make **kayaks** and **umiaks** so they might sail and hunt on the water.

Yet the people grew into many, as did the animals, and they were crowded on their small island. Only the sea was big.

One day an enormous black monster, unlike any other animal, rose from the sea. The people rowed to it in their kayaks and umiaks and tried to harpoon it, but none of the harpoons could pierce the monster's thick skin.

The raven watched the people's hopeless fight and said to the little sparrow, "Come with me and hover over the monster; I am going to hunt it in a kayak."

The raven paddled out, and while the sparrow hovered in the air, the raven harpooned and killed the monster.

The people rejoiced and towed the monster back to their village. They cut the body into small pieces and threw the pieces in all directions. Out in the sea, many islands grew from these pieces until they formed a great and enormous coast. Now there was room for the people and the animals. The raven called all the people together and spoke to them: "I am your father. To me you owe your lives and your land. You must never forget me."

Then he flew into the sky. There he flung the rest of the mica, and light shot across the world like a great fire. Thus were sky and the earth created.

This was the creation of the world and its people and the animals, but before all this came the raven, and before him the little sparrow.

For thousands of years, the Inuit have inhabited broad expanses of the Arctic and Subarctic from eastern Siberia across North America to Greenland. Cleverly adapting to the environment, largely through hunting and fishing, they have thrived in a world of ice and bleak **tundra**—a land where the temperature can plunge to –80 degrees Fahrenheit (–62 degrees Celsius). One community in Etah, Greenland, is located just 900 miles (1,448 kilometers) from the North Pole and is the northernmost human settlement on Earth.

The homeland of the Inuit spans four nations— Greenland, Canada, Russia, and the coastal areas of Alaska. For centuries, the Inuit were known to the outside world as Eskimos, an Algonquian word once thought to mean "eaters of raw flesh." It is now believed that the obscure name may actually refer to

Polar bear tracks in the snow near Hudson Bay in Nunavut, Canada

snowshoes. In any case, the people refer to themselves as Inuit, which means "the people."

It is generally believed that the Inuit moved on foot and by dogsled across the Bering Strait from Siberia to North America between 3000 and 1000 BCE, long after the ancestors of other Native North American peoples had migrated to the continent. Other scholars believe the time of migration may have been much earlier—between 6000 and 5000 BCE. The oldest known villages, dating from about 2000 BCE, have been found on the Aleutian Islands off the coast of the United States and in southwestern Alaska. The Inuit gradually spread eastward into northern Canada and Greenland.

The People and Culture of the Inuit

Living over such a vast region, the Inuit came to be divided into three large groups: the Alaska Inuit, which includes the Yuik of Siberia; the Central Inuit, which includes those in northern Canada, Labrador, and Baffin Island; and the Greenland Inuit. The Central Inuit in Canada include peoples, such as the Labrador Inuit, who make their home on the coast across from Newfoundland to Hudson Bay and on southern Baffin Island. The Central Inuit also live on the far northern areas of Greenland, on Baffin Island, and around Hudson Bay. The Banks Island Inuit, a Central Inuit group, inhabit Banks Island, Victoria Island, and the other islands along Canada's central Arctic coast. The Mackenzie River Inuit, also a Central Inuit group, have long made their home along the Arctic coast of western Canada.

An iceberg looms in the distance in Baffin Bay.

Preserving Tradition

The Inuit speak several closely related languages in the Eskimoan language family. Eskimoan itself is divided into two branches, Sirenikski-Yupik and Inuit-Inupiaq. Sirenikski and Yupik are spoken in Siberia. Yupik is also spoken in southwestern Alaska. People in northern Alaska speak Inupiaq. In Canada the language is called Inuit, and in Greenland, Greenlandic.

In most parts of Greenland, as in Canada, the Native word for "people" is *inuit*, but Greenlanders today generally refer to themselves as *Kalaallitt*, a term of Danish origin meaning the native people of Greenland. These various names continue to be used. However, in 1977, the international Native organization known as the Inuit Circumpolar Council (then called the Inuit Circumpolar Conference) adopted local usages, and the term "Inuit" has gained wide acceptance.

Although there are regional variations in the Inuit way of life, many traditions remain unchanged. For example, they have traditionally hunted, trapped, and fished. Today, as in the past, men hunt, fish, and build homes, while women make clothing and cook meals. The Inuit eat seals, walruses, whales, fish, and **muktuk**, the layer of fat under a whale's skin. They also hunt caribou, polar bears, and smaller mammals such as arctic foxes and snowshoe hares. The eggs and meat of ducks, geese, and seabirds are also eaten. Food is often frozen and eaten cooked or dried. Seals, especially important to many Inuit, provide food, skins for clothes, meat for sled dogs, and oil for fuel. The Inuit use practically every part of the animal—skins for clothes, homes, and boats; bones for weapons and tools. Before a hunt, people hold ceremonies in hopes of finding game, and they honor the animals that they have killed in rituals.

When they first arrived in North America, the Inuit created a culture of survival that affected every aspect of life. People struggled to secure the food, clothing, and shelter necessary to survive under the very harsh conditions of the Arctic land, sea, and weather. The culture included language, arts, and games, along with singing, dancing, and storytelling. Parents and grandparents taught their children the skills and beliefs needed to endure and enjoy the cold reaches of the north.

For many generations, families have made their homes on stretches of flat, barren, and often windswept land in an unforgiving climate. Parents and unmarried children, as well as married sons and their wives and children, once lived together to ensure a better chance of surviving. Today, many such traditions remain in place. For example, the head of the family is the oldest man able to hunt. During the winter, several families often come together in a settlement. However, during the summer, the families go their separate ways to hunt and fish.

In ancient times, homes varied by region. In Greenland and Alaska, the Inuit formed villages of stone or **igloos**. Igloo is an Inuit word meaning "house." They are still used today. Depending on the season, igloos are made of walrus or sealskin, or blocks of snow. During the winter, the Inuit of central and eastern Canada have traditionally lived in dome-shaped igloos made of snow blocks. In Siberia, they constructed houses with driftwood and soil.

An Inuit family poses outside their igloo.

The Inuit's skill in making homes, tools, weapons, and clothing from the often scarce materials available to them has enabled them to survive in the harsh land and climate of the north over the generations.

People travel over water in kayaks and umiaks. Covered with the skins of caribou or seals, a kayak carries one person who sits in an opening in the center of the long, closed boat. Gliding through the water in a kayak,

The People and Culture of the Inuit

a hunter can silently approach prey. Made of a wooden frame covered with walrus skins, an umiak is a large, open boat. The Inuit use umiaks to carry people and supplies on hunting trips. People rely on dogsleds pulled by a team of as many as fourteen huskies to journey over the snow-covered land and frozen water. Today, many Inuit use motorized boats and snowmobiles as well.

Connecting to the Land

The great sea
Has sent me adrift,
It moves me as the weed in a great river,
Earth and the great weather
Move me,
Have carried me away
And move my inward parts with joy.

For many people, the Arctic is a cold and forbidding place, sprawling about 3,200 miles (5,150 km) from Greenland across the expanse of northern Canada and the northern coast of Alaska to the eastern Aleutian Islands. Yet the Inuit have sustained themselves for generations in this seemingly bleak landscape that stretches from Siberia to Greenland, and from southeastern Labrador to the Queen Elizabeth Islands. The vast territory also embraces more than 2,000 miles (3,219 km) of northern Alaskan coast and the Aleutian Island chain that extends more than 1,000 miles (1,609 km) from southern Alaska. A substantial Native Inuit population exists in these areas today, the largest populations being in Greenland and Denmark, with a total of 70,000, and in Canada, with 59,000.

Navigating Climate

Temperatures are eased somewhat along the coast of the Pacific Ocean and nearby waters, although unrelenting winds blast the coast. In most of the Arctic, however, winters are long, dark, and bitterly cold, and the tundra is blanketed with a hard crust of ice and snow. Although some Inuit—especially in western Alaska—live in forested areas, most communities are well north of the timberline. Hugging the ground, dwarf flowers, mosses, and lichens flourish during the brief warmth and light of summer. During the summer, the flat land is usually spongy due to poor drainage and permafrost, a layer of ice beneath the surface that never thaws. Mosquitoes, black flies, and other biting insects breed in the shallow pools of water that collect on the tundra. Rising up in great, blood-sucking swarms, the mosquitoes attack people and caribou.

Despite all the ice and snow that collects on the surface, most of the Arctic is actually an arid region with as little as four inches of precipitation a year. The exceptions are in Labrador and southwestern Alaska, which receive a good bit of rain carried by the ocean winds. For water, the Inuit rely on ocean ice, which loses much of its salt content after a year or so of being frozen. Otherwise, the Inuit and other Native peoples of the far north would never have enough freshwater.

Living primarily along the coastline and offshore islands, the Inuit became skilled hunters on land and sea. They came to understand the subtle changes in the land, sea, and ice that made up their world. Their quarry included sea mammals, notably seals, walruses, narwhals, and whales. While seals were essential to the

The People and Culture of the Inuit

A group of Alaska Inuit villagers drag a walrus to their village, circa 1930.

survival of some Inuit groups, caribou were the most vital source of food for others, especially during spring and autumn migrations of the caribou. The Inuit hunted other land mammals for meat or fur. They also shot birds and gathered eggs from nests. In some regions of the north, they picked berries. They caught large numbers of fish with hooks, nets, spears, and traps.

The Inuit have a history that spans centuries. They have overcome obstacles of weather, animal, and human encounters. Over the centuries, they have connected with the land and are aware of the power it possesses in their remote area. Though their homeland is in one of the world's harshest environments, they have found many ways not only to survive but also to establish a flourishing culture. Their enduring nature is uplifting and is one of the aspects for which people admire them today.

This illustration from Captain Ross's voyage narrative, written between 1829 and 1833, shows one representation of early Inuit people.

[Inuit knowledge] is intricate, complex. They live very close to nature.

—On Thin Ice, NBC documentary

BUILDING A CIVILIZATION

Once the Inuit's ancestors had arrived on North American soil, they quickly realized that in order to survive they needed to understand the land. Forming groups, the Inuit migrated northward and eventually established communities amidst the cold and snowy terrain. These communities evolved over time. Various customs, rituals, and beliefs were formed. Today, some of these traditions remain a part of Inuit life.

An Inuit family sits outside the Hudson's Bay Company's trading post on Southampton Island in the Northwest Territories.

Family Life

The Inuit traditionally lived in small, isolated villages scattered widely over the snowy expanses. Some villages may have had as many as eight hundred inhabitants, especially if game was abundant in the region. However, most communities consisted of groups of ten to fifty people who were usually related by blood or marriage. Each of these camps had one to six dwellings in which men, women, and children lived together.

Because they had to devote so much time and energy to hunting and protecting themselves from the bitter cold, the Inuit did not form complex social and political organizations. The basic social unit was the family, which usually consisted of the husband and the wife and their two or three children. At one time, it

The People and Culture of the Inuit

was thought that the small number of children in Inuit families was due to **infanticide** or a high infant mortality rate because of the harsh climate. However, it is more likely that Inuit women simply had fewer children for a number of reasons. Women breast-fed their children until they were five or six years old—or sometimes even older. While breast-feeding, they were less likely to get pregnant again. Due to food shortages and the rigors of life, women also had greater difficulty in getting pregnant, or they frequently had miscarriages, especially when they undertook arduous travel and tasks, such as hauling and butchering caribou and other large animals. In the early twentieth century, as the Inuit became more settled and women began to wean their children at a younger age, the birth rate increased.

Occasionally, some Inuit did allow a newborn to die, especially if harsh conditions made it impossible to care for the baby. They let the baby freeze to death, but only before they had given it a name, since they believed that a body without a name was not yet a human being. However, such measures were undertaken only in the most desperate situations, for example, when the family was facing starvation. At all other times, children were cherished as a way to continue the life of the family, provide care for parents in old age, and to bring joy to their families. Both the very old and the very young enhanced the community. The Inuit loved to be surrounded by other people, especially other family members. Living together for years, often in close quarters, people knew each other so well that a slight gesture or change in expression could communicate a thought or feeling.

Family life could become very complicated, especially when the fifty or so people in a settlement were all members of a single family. Traditionally, people relied on their extended families. Many men had two or three wives and, in some regions, women occasionally had two husbands. Because of the multiple marriages, relationships became even more complicated. Inuit families had fewer children and more adult relatives than typical Western families. Relatives and in-laws often acted as though they were members of a nuclear family of parents and children. Cousins often viewed each other as brother and sister. Aunts and uncles often treated nieces and nephews as their own children.

Elders were honored for their wisdom and knowledge of customs and **taboos**, as well as for their skill as storytellers. Many Westerners once thought that the Inuit viewed the elderly as a burden. It is true that during a famine an aged person might wander out into a snowstorm to freeze to death, so that the small amount of food on hand would be left for the young and strong. When people moved to another hunting ground, an old person who could no longer carry heavy loads might also decide to be left behind. However, the Inuit valued the lives of everyone in the community. They believed that death was a passing of the soul from one body to another. When an old woman sacrificed herself to the freezing cold, people believed that her soul would soon come back in a newborn baby. The family gave her name to the next baby born, and in the ensuing weeks, people might note how the infant displayed traits and manners similar to those of the old woman. To the Inuit, all lives were bound in an ever-renewing cycle.

Government

Family members formed especially strong cooperative bonds as they worked together to provide food, clothing, and shelter. Hunters were honored to share their meat with others in the group. If one group went on a hunting expedition and abandoned a house, others were allowed to seek shelter there. However, the Inuit sense of cooperation posed difficulties in relating with Europeans. The Inuit generally trusted other people and thus were often cheated by dishonest traders. When it came to dealing with the nations that claimed sovereignty over them, the Inuit, without a strong political organization, often could not understand the language and treaty terms, let alone negotiate with the representatives of these governments.

The Inuit did rely on strong leaders and a hierarchical structure within the family in managing their daily lives. Parents had authority over their children. Elders also generally had more influence over younger members of the group, although they served primarily as advisers. The men made most of the decisions, especially when moving the camp. However, this authority was often expressed through respect rather than orders. For instance, a father might say, "We are getting low on seal meat," instead of directly telling his son to go hunting. If a father said, "I'm thirsty," that meant the younger son was expected to fetch him a drink of water.

People traced their descent through both sides of their family. Kinship was critically important. Strangers who could not establish their relationship with the group were considered hostile and might even be killed. Yet cooperation was also necessary and unrelated people often came together to hunt, trade, and even avenge a death. They also enjoyed visiting other families. They often came together to play games and share stories, as well as to hold festivals and feasts, all of which strengthened the bonds of unity. Sometimes, men exchanged their wives for brief periods of time. Families shared the labor of moving to new hunting grounds.

Housing

Depending on where they lived, the Inuit made two kinds of winter homes. Central Inuit usually built snow igloos. They often attached several igloos for greater warmth and to provide separate areas for living, sleeping, and storage. Men first cut blocks of wind-hardened snow and laid the blocks as a foundation, a circle about 10 to 15 feet (3 to 4.6 meters) in diameter. They then stacked rows of blocks, each succeeding row placed slightly inward to make a dome shape.

An Inuit woman cuts blubber off the skin of a white whale, circa 1924.

They briefly melted the surface of the inside wall with the heat of a **blubber** lamp known as a **kudlik**. The surface quickly froze again into a windproof glaze. The Inuit often added a small porch for storage and a window of clear ice. For ventilation, they left a small hole at the top of the dome. To enter or exit the snow house, people crawled through a long, low tunnel that kept cold air from blowing into the house. Inside, they made benches and tables of hard-packed snow. Platforms covered with warm furs and willow branches, if available, served as beds. For light and heat, women tended a small blubber lamp over which they placed a cooking pot or drying rack.

An igloo in Manitoba, Canada, set against an Arctic sunset

Igloos were common, especially among the Inuit who lived in northern Canada, where snow is plentiful. However, many people used igloos only as temporary shelters. Most Inuit, especially those living in Greenland and Alaska, constructed a square or oblong house known as a **karmat**. These earth dwellings consisted of a wood or whalebone frame built over a shallow pit. The frame was covered with sod. As with an igloo, people entered through a tunnel, although in some regions, they used a passageway through the roof. Occasionally they stretched clear animal gut over small openings to make windows. Another important building was a large ceremonial house for the men, which was known in western Alaska as the **kashim**. During the summer, the Inuit lived in tents made by covering driftwood or whalebone frames with seal or caribou skins.

The People and Culture of the Inuit

Although the Inuit tradition of building igloos remains today, it is not the only option for dwellings. Many Inuit communities today use igloos as a tourist attraction or for show. Still, igloos serve an interesting purpose even now. Keeping with tradition, an Inuit man cannot marry unless he knows how to build an igloo.

As the Inuit progressed as a culture and community, weathering the harsh environmental conditions, they preserved their traditions and stories through word of mouth and careful instruction. Their communities eventually became stationary, and today the Inuit spend much of their lives living in the same local areas, no longer having to migrate to find food. They have become an integral part of Native American society.

This photo shows an old Inuit kashim, or dance house.

A small Alaskan village sits near an estuary, circa 1955.

CHAPTER THREE

Originally ... throat singing was a form of entertainment among Inuit women while the men were away on hunting trips.

—*Explore: Arctic Inuit Culture, 2013*

LIFE IN THE INUIT NATION

Life for the early Inuit people was difficult. In order to survive, they formed family or communal units. This way, men and women could work together to construct buildings, to hunt, and to provide for each other. For the Inuit, community life was important. It joined people together and ensured they could continue living in difficult conditions. If a man had no wife to sew and cook for him, he became a burden to his family. Without good clothes, he froze when he hunted in the winter. Without a husband, a woman had no one to provide meat for meals and hides for clothes. When a man and woman married, they were able to help each other. Their children also helped to provide for the family. The success of future generations depended on raising healthy and strong individuals who were able to provide for themselves and each other.

The Life Cycle

Every day, the Inuit celebrated the life they had been given. Their practices and traditions concerning life and death were unique to the tribe. They had different rituals for the birth of a baby, marrying, and when someone died. Altogether, these elements formed everyday life for the men, women, and children who belonged to the Inuit community.

Being Born

During pregnancy, a woman often worried about the uncertain future. Would the baby come during a blizzard or a time of starvation when people were migrating over the tundra? Would she have a boy who would take care of her in old age or a girl for whom she would have to find a good match someday? Would she and the baby live or perish during childbirth?

If the woman went into labor on the trail, she would drop behind and have her baby, sometimes alone. She tried to have the baby as quickly as possible and then catch up with the others. While she recovered, the new mother was allowed to ride in a sled with her baby tucked warmly inside the **amaut**, or hood, of her coat.

An Inuit mother and child wear modern dress.

Yet, in most instances, the woman did not give birth
alone. Her husband and one or two women, serving
as midwives, helped with the delivery. If there were
complications, a shaman, or **angakok**, was brought in to
ask the spirits, or **inuas**, for help.

The woman gave birth in a kneeling position. If the
group was not on the move, she rested indoors for
several days to regain her strength. During this time, her
other children were sent to stay with friends or family.
The Inuit observed various taboos after a child was
born. The mother had to make a fire under a cooking
pot as soon as possible—to ensure that her child would

learn to walk at an early age. A friend or relative also stretched the legs to help the child grow tall. Whenever the mother ate she had to rub a little food on her baby's cheek to ensure that he or she would never go hungry.

The mother of a newborn could not eat from the common pot. She had to have her own cooking pot and bowl. Her cooking pot could not be traded or given away until her child was fully grown. Similarly, the baby's first ritual clothing, often a caribou skin robe, was carefully stored away. The umbilical cord was kept as an **amulet**. If any of these objects were to be lost, it was believed that the child would die.

The Inuit always remembered the day on which a child was born. They recalled everyone who was present at the birth. They knew if a snowstorm had been raging or if the dogs had been howling in the wind that day. All of these details formed the first chapter of a person's life story.

Babies usually wore no clothes except for an animal skin diaper. For the first few months, they were kept warm and safe inside the amaut of their mother's coat. Children did not receive their first clothes—a one-piece suit with a flap in the back for diaper changing—until they were old enough to walk. Mittens, which were attached to the suit, and sealskin shoes completed the outfit.

Parents cherished their babies. A mother snuggled her infant within her heavy coat. She carried her baby wherever she went. The baby slept with her and breast-fed whenever it was hungry for at least three years but usually longer. As the Inuit's diet is composed mostly of meat, weaning was gradual. The mother first gave broth and boiled fish to her baby. Later, she fed the infant seal or caribou meat that she had chewed.

Growing Up

Most Inuit named their children immediately after birth, although some people waited a few days. Friends and family suggested names to the parents, who generally named their child after a relative who had recently passed away. Most people had two names. Sometimes a person was called one name by the family and another name by outsiders. Occasionally people acquired nicknames as well.

Although they were often busy, parents attentively cared for their children and seldom punished them. Children had the run of the camp, where they were generally safe, as everyone knew them and helped watch over them. Parents instructed their children to be

An Inuit couple hunts with bows and arrows.

patient and cheerful. Obedience and hard work were encouraged by everyone in the community.

Children learned many important skills needed for survival. Mothers taught their daughters how to cook meals and sew clothing. Fathers taught their sons—and occasionally their daughters—how to hunt and fish. Parents lavished praise on their children when they excelled at any of these tasks.

Children also played with toys, such as little sleds to which they harnessed puppies. With their own small-scale bows and arrows, they practiced archery by shooting at blocks of snow. They pretended to drive caribou into pits and used sticks for kayaks. Girls enjoyed playing with dolls. They also sewed with needles and tended toy lamps made from small pieces of soapstone. In Alaska, a father often carved a "story knife" for his daughter from a walrus tusk or driftwood. As she drew pictures of animals, people, and everyday activities in the snow, the girl made up stories that she shared with her friends.

Maturing

The warm clothing—parka, trousers, boots—was important not only for cold weather but also for spiritual protection as children grew up. The Inuit often sewed amulets to their clothes to ward off evil spirits and provide guidance. For instance, it was believed that a flipper bone from a ringed seal would help a young man become a good hunter. A piece of fish skin assisted a young woman in becoming skilled at sewing. Other amulets included the hair of an old man to ensure long life, a raven skin to make a person invisible when hunting, and the head of a red-throated loon to help in fishing. Boys also often grew their hair long as protection against spiritual dangers.

Girls generally wore the same kind of clothes until they were married. Boys usually began to wear men's clothing when they came of age and began to hunt and fish with their fathers.

Marrying

Girls typically married before their first menstrual period. In marriage, romance mattered less than the skills of a woman and the hunting ability of the man. Sometimes marriages were arranged in advance by the parents, but young people were not bound to these betrothals. When they came of age, they could marry whomever they wished. There was no special wedding ceremony. The couple simply decided to live together.

Dying

Inuit life was hard, and few people lived to old age. Men usually died in their mid-forties and women in their mid-fifties. For the few people who lived long enough, old age was considered a misery. Sometimes crippled, toothless, and nearly blind, old people became a burden to themselves and their families. When food was scarce and people had to move camp, an elderly mother or father might stay behind in a little snow house that served as both shelter and tomb. Similarly, during hard times, baby girls were occasionally left to die in the snow because the family could not afford to keep them. Boys were spared because they would ultimately grow old enough to become hunters who

This photo shows a cross, with writing in Inuit, which marks the grave of a child.

could provide game and fish. Among some groups, such as the Caribou Inuit of central Canada, women outnumbered men because of the high male mortality through hunting accidents.

The Inuit respected and feared the dead. They believed that the spirit of the deceased would become evil and seek revenge on the living. It was thought that dead people who had not been treated properly hated the living and brought winter storms and starvation. Among one Inuit group, the Copper Inuit, the body of the deceased was bound with thongs to keep its spirit from harming others. Following the death of a man, the body lay in a house or tent for three days. If a woman died, her body lay for four days. During this time people mourned and observed many taboos. They could not sew or comb their hair. At night they laid knives between the body and the rest of the household, perhaps to protect themselves as they slept from the dead person's spirit.

After the period of mourning, a hole was cut in the back wall of the house or tent, and the body was removed. It was believed that no other spirits should observe the family taking away the deceased. The house and belongings of the deceased were then abandoned. Unable to dig a grave in the rocky, frozen ground, people laid the body in a circle of small stones and covered it with stones and driftwood. The Copper Inuit, however, left the body uncovered. They cut the thongs that bound the body to release the spirit of the dead person. Finally, they placed some or all of the deceased's belongings with the body for use in the afterlife.

After the funeral, anyone who had handled the body had to drink water when they arrived home, so the deceased would not be thirsty. They also had to give a piece of blubber from the first animal killed after the burial to every person in the village. Each person then burned the blubber in a lamp.

Some Inuit had taboos against speaking the dead person's name. They occasionally visited the grave. However, if the person had died violently, they believed the grave might be haunted by an evil spirit and they stayed away.

Fishing and Hunting

With few edible plants in the Arctic, the Inuit sustained themselves mostly by hunting and fishing. Men spent most of each day in pursuit of whales, seals, or caribou. They also hunted walruses, sea lions, and narwhals that had migrated north in the warmer months.

Whether hunting seals or whales, men used basically the same equipment—harpoons to which lines and air-filled sealskin floats were attached. Sometimes, a man working alone could spear a small whale or seal from his kayak. Along the Pacific coast of Alaska, men speared whales with poison-tipped lances, then went home and undertook rituals intended to kill the whale magically. Other men watched the whale as it swam through the water. As the poison worked through its body, the whale eventually died, but often far away from where it had been speared. Whales speared by hunters in one village often floated to the surface or washed ashore near another village. However, as whales were plentiful, there was enough food for everyone living along the coast.

In the eastern Arctic, groups of men in kayaks hunted large bowhead whales. Each man tried to thrust a harpoon into the whale's head. Exhausted by dragging many floats, the whale had to surface, at which point the men attempted to kill it with spears. However, men were often able to thrust only one or two harpoons, and many whales escaped.

In Greenland and northwestern Alaska, men hunted more effectively in crews paddling umiaks. Each crew usually had six paddlers, a harpooner, and a helmsman who steered the boat. Unlike a single hunter who had to paddle and steer his kayak while trying to throw a harpoon, each man in the umiak could concentrate on his assigned task. Using both hands, the harpooner drove a sturdy harpoon into the whale in a powerful and precise thrust. Three or four floats were attached to the harpoon to ensure that the whale would soon tire.

The Inuit beliefs and traditions connect them to the land and sea.

When exhausted from dragging the floats, the whale surfaced. Men then speared the whale and towed its body to shore.

In parts of Alaska and southwestern Greenland, the ocean never freezes. However, everywhere else in the polar north, the sea freezes for at least half of the year. During the winter, when boats could not be used, men usually hunted seals from ice floes, waiting at breathing holes called **aglus**. Sea mammals have to periodically come up for air and hunters often relied on a dog to sniff out the breathing holes that were usually covered with snow and nearly invisible. Since larger sea mammals migrated southward, the Inuit mainly hunted seals during the winter. Floats dragged by harpooned animals, called drag floats, could not be used on the ice, so men had to harpoon the seal directly in the head. Men hunted as a group, each patiently guarding one of the many holes in the ice. A man might watch his breathing hole for hours in the dark and intense cold for a single, fleeting chance

Seals are among the animals that Inuit hunt to survive.

to catch a single seal. In warmer seasons, the men stalked seals on the ice or harpooned them from kayaks.

A man waited hours, often days, for a seal to bob up in a breathing hole. If he missed, he would have to begin the vigil all over again. Some people, such as the Copper Inuit of the central Arctic, hunted in groups. Moving the entire village onto the ice a few miles from shore, they placed a hunter at each breathing hole. If every breathing hole was covered, a seal was likely to be caught by at least one hunter. When most of the seals had been hunted at one location, the village moved to another site.

When the sun began to appear again in the spring, seals began to crawl out onto the ice and warm themselves next to their breathing holes. Raising their heads every minute or so, the seals kept careful watch. A hunter had to crawl over the ice on his belly, pretending

The People and Culture of the Inuit

to be another seal. When the seal raised its head, the hunter either lay perfectly still like a seal sunning itself or raised his head like a seal looking around. He might stalk a seal for several hours only to see the seal slip into the water when he was just a few yards away. Or he might be lucky enough to spear the seal with his harpoon.

Hunting was often dangerous. Bowhead whales could easily capsize an umiak with a single sweep of their tails. Humpback and gray whales of the Pacific even attacked small boats. With their sharp tusks, walruses were especially dangerous. Although smaller than most whales, a bull walrus can still weigh more than an entire umiak crew—and a bull walrus is quite fierce. It will viciously charge not only a man hunting alone but also large boats. Walruses also gather in pods of dozens or even hundreds of animals, so hunting had to be undertaken with the utmost care. Even then, hunters were often killed by these aggressive mammals.

In many areas, such as the interior of northwestern Alaska, the **barrens** west of Hudson Bay, and stretches of land in northern Canada, the caribou was the Inuit's main source of food. Also known as the North American reindeer, caribou provided not only meat but also hides for shelter, clothing, and boats, as well as **sinew** for thread. Large numbers of these animals migrated across the northern part of the mainland, while smaller herds lived in the ice-free areas of Greenland and on many of the islands of northern Canada.

Always on the move, caribou wintered south of the timberline and migrated to the tundra during warmer weather. When the herds returned north in the summer, men ambushed them—either by creeping up or hiding in a pit until the caribou passed by. They could never be sure of the route to be taken by the caribou, but they observed weather conditions and consulted with shamans. They also knew that caribou frequented certain routes, such as shallow river crossings and valleys through hills and mountains. Cooperating in group hunts, men stacked piles of rocks, or cairns, in a large V shape that narrowed at the edge of the water or a corral. As the caribou approached the wide part of the V, women and children, who had been in hiding, shouted and waved their arms, driving the herd into the V. If the cairns ended at a river, men waiting in kayaks speared or shot the caribou with bows and arrows as they plunged into the current. After they had killed enough animals, they retrieved the carcasses floating in the water. If the cairns were located on land, the Inuit built a corral at the narrow end and caught the caribou there with snares made of the skins of walruses or seals.

Fish were also a vital source of food, especially to the Inuit of Alaska. Men caught fish with hooks and lines, nets, and spears. Many Alaskan Inuit fished all winter with gill nets placed under the ice. Fish, such as the Arctic cod in areas of Alaska and the capelin of the Atlantic, from time to time washed ashore in large numbers. People simply had to scoop them up in baskets. Favorite kinds of freshwater fish included trout, grayling, blackfish, and pike. People caught halibut, tomcod, capelin, herring, and sharks in the ocean. In southwestern Alaska, people also caught eels. The most important fish were those that migrated from the sea to freshwater, such as Arctic char and several kinds of whitefish and salmon. To catch migratory fish, the

Inuit often built **weirs**. These weirs consisted of two stone dams or fences across the river where the fish were ascending. An opening was left in the lower, or downstream, dam. When enough fish had swum through the opening and were blocked by the second weir, men closed the opening. People then waded into the water and speared the fish. Instead of weirs, people in the western Arctic—usually women—used nets made of lines of sealskin, willow bark, or shredded baleen to catch migrating fish.

Pacific salmon die after **spawning**, but char and Atlantic salmon, after wintering in lakes and rivers, head to the sea again in early summer. Some Inuit caught fish during these migrations. In the western Arctic, whitefish and freshwater grayling move downriver in the autumn. To catch these fish, some Inuit built a fence with a narrow gate across a stream. They placed a basket with a cone-shaped opening over the gate. Fish swam into the basket but then could not easily swim out again. The construction of the fence required considerable labor, but afterward the fisherman only had to periodically raise and empty the basket filled with fish.

Depending on where they lived, Inuit bands hunted many other kinds of animals besides seals and caribou. These included musk oxen, mountain sheep, grizzly bears, polar bears, lynxes, wolves, wolverines, and foxes. Depending on the place and the season, they also caught sea otters, river otters, muskrats, marmots, hares, and ground squirrels. Over many generations, men perfected their methods and weapons for catching these animals. They hunted them from blinds and trapped them in snares, deadfalls, and weighted nets.

They also used three or four kinds of arrows, as well as a dozen varied kinds of spears or harpoons, each of which was ideally suited for hunting a particular mammal, bird, or fish.

To supplement their diet, some Inuit also harvested crabs, shellfish, and sea urchins. During the spring and summer, they gathered the eggs of ducks, geese, swans, and seabirds nesting in the cliffs. Snowy owls were occasionally cooked in soups, and in some locales ptarmigan were a source of food during the late winter. Yet the Inuit's survival largely depended on their ability to gather and store large amounts of meat and fish during brief summer seasons. Whether whale, seal, or caribou, the meat was fairly divided among the people according to time-honored rules. The Inuit cut the flesh into strips and allowed them to dry for two or three days. In the far north they stored frozen carcasses under piles of rocks. The Inuit of Alaska dug pits that served as cellars in the frozen ground. People often ate fish and meat raw and cooked only the toughest pieces. The Inuit never wasted any part of their fish and game. They ate the flesh and used the skins and bones to make tools, weapons, and shelters. Blubber was an especially important resource for light, heat, and medicine, as well as for food. Stored out of direct sunlight, cubes of seal blubber melted into a clear liquid similar to vegetable oil. Melted blubber was eaten and burned in lamps for heat and light. When game was scarce, the Inuit might have to eat their clothing or even their dogs. The word *ajurnamat*, which means "it cannot be helped," reflects the Inuit's patience and acceptance of fate. However, during good times they enjoyed great feasts.

The People and Culture of the Inuit

Cooking

The Inuit believed that food tasted better when shared with family and friends. Sharing reminded people of the critical need for cooperation. When people ate together, they felt a deeper sense of appreciation for everyone around them. Strangers became friends when offered a meal. Celebrations centered around a great feast with lots of fresh meat or frozen fish that had been **cached** for the long, sunless days of winter. At these gatherings, people chatted, laughed, and told stories. To this day, people enjoy coming together for community feasts that include plenty of traditional foods. Everyone gathers in a public place to enjoy food donated by different families. In larger communities, much of the food is provided by specially chosen hunters.

In one feast, known as *alupajaq*, the Inuit continue to honor the traditions of their ancestors. The men gather around a seal that is to be eaten. Two or three men ritually cut up the animal, while the women remain in a group several feet away. They listen as the men tell hunting stories. The women talk happily about the seal and the good fortune of being blessed with plenty. The meat is passed from the men to the women, with the choicest parts given to the women. First come the upper flippers, which two women cut into pieces for everyone. Slivers of the heart are then passed around the group. These are followed by the liver. The tender meat on the upper spine is shared by the women while the men take the meat from the lower spine. The women next accept the front ribs and the men take the back ribs. Guests take care to leave part of the seal for their generous

SEAFOOD CHOWDER

Here is a modern recipe that includes fish and other ingredients traditionally eaten by the Inuit.

INGREDIENTS

1.5 cups (355 milliliters) clams

2.5 pounds (1.1 kilograms) assorted fish cubed (halibut, salmon, cod, or other fish)

0.5 cups (118 mL) shelled crab meat

5 strips bacon

2 onions, finely chopped

2 stalks of finely chopped celery

6 to 8 medium-sized potatoes, peeled and cubed

2 cans chicken broth

0.5 teaspoons (3 mL) salt

0.25 teaspoons (1.5 mL) pepper

1 can evaporated milk

1 cup (237 mL) milk

8 tablespoons (142 mL) of flour

Dice the bacon and fry in a large pot until crisp and brown. Add chicken broth, onion, celery, clams, crab, potatoes, and seasonings. Bring mixture to a boil and cook until potatoes are tender. Add cubed fish and simmer for five minutes. Be careful not to overcook the fish.

Blend flour, evaporated milk, and regular milk. Pour this mixture into pot and heat until the chowder thickens. Do not allow the liquid to come to a boil. Add additional pepper to taste and serve.

hosts, although they are often encouraged to take some of the meat home. Expressing their thanks, some guests politely leave as soon as they have eaten, even before washing up. They do not wish to take up too much room and overstay their welcome. The remaining guests help in cleaning up after the meal.

Traditionally, the Inuit ate meat frozen or with a variety of sauces, such as *aalu*, *misiraq*, and *nirukkaq* as flavorings. Aalu was—and still is—made from lean, choice cuts of caribou or seal meat that have been cut into small pieces and mixed with a little melted fat, animal blood, and ptarmigan intestine. Women mix the ingredients briskly with their fingers until it becomes frothy. Aalu is one of the most popular dips for many kinds of meat. Misiraq is made from seal or whale blubber. Stored in a cool place, the blubber is allowed to age until it becomes a clear, aromatic liquid. Nirukkaq is made with the contents of a caribou stomach that have been frozen, thawed, and cleaned of bits of grass and lichens. People use nirukkaq as a dip for caribou meat.

Traditionally, the Inuit also ate dried fish and meats, such as caribou. By strict custom, caribou stew had to be prepared on land. The dish was often cooked with blackberry canes to give the meat a pleasant woody smell and taste. Over the past century, the Inuit have adapted new recipes for caribou and fish that include spices. The Inuit also occasionally ate greens such as chard, if they were available. They gathered wild potatoes, flowers, and berries, and dug the roots of some plants. However, their diet consisted mainly of meat and fats that provided the strength and energy needed to hunt and fish in the intense cold.

Clothes and Accessories

The Alaska Inuit who lived in the mild climate along the Pacific coast had to contend with rain and wind but not much cold. They dressed lightly in a long pullover shirt with a high collar and a tightly fitting neck. Over the shirt, they often wore a hooded, waterproof windbreaker known as a kamleika. However, most Inuit had to wear clothing suitable for the intense cold of the north, or they would quickly freeze to death.

Basic attire included a hooded parka, heavy trousers, boots, and mittens. Although men and women wore the same outfits, the styles varied between the sexes. In some regions, women's pants and boots were sewn together to make one garment. Women made summer clothes of waterproof sealskin and winter clothes of warm, yet lightweight caribou hide. They also used the fur of other animals, including polar bears, wolves, foxes, dogs, marmots, and squirrels, as well as bird feathers, in making clothing. In the winter, people generally wore two garments—an inner suit with the fur turned toward the skin and an outer parka with the fur out. Parkas fit snugly around the wrists, waist, and neck to keep out the cold. Women's parkas occasionally included a warm, fur-lined amaut to carry babies. Called **mukluks** or **kamiks**, boots had moss or down between each of four layers of caribou hide or sealskin for warmth. Women's boots went all the way up the thigh, while men's boots were shorter.

Early explorers thought the Inuit were fat, but their bulky clothing only made them appear to be heavy. The layers of winter clothing were so remarkably warm that the Inuit could sleep outdoors, in an outfit weighing only

The Inuit make their own clothes, including thick fur coats made from the animals they hunt.

about 10 pounds (4.5 kg), even when the temperature plunged to –60 degrees Fahrenheit (–51 degrees C). The clothing was so well insulated that it became a shelter when men went on hunting trips for two or three days. At night, they simply built a windbreak of snow and hunkered down inside their warm parkas.

From an early age, women learned to sew the seams of clothing tightly with sinew so that garments would repel water. In the Arctic, staying dry was essential. A person who got wet quickly froze to death. However, the clothing was so well sewn that it could not breathe. Moisture, including perspiration, condensed on the skin, so the Inuit had to continually dry their clothing. As soon as they came from a hunt, men brushed the snow off their clothes before entering the warm home. Once inside, they quickly shed the outside layer of their clothing, which the women turned inside out and carefully dried over a blubber lamp. Women then chewed the boots and beat other clothes with a stick if they had gotten stiff.

People dressed for special occasions in clothing trimmed with fur and embroidered with designs. Among the Copper Inuit, men's dance regalia was often adorned with lemming skins. Women often had an extensive wardrobe that included both everyday clothes and fancier dance outfits. Many people wore *atagtat*, or amulets, as sacred objects on their clothing to bring good fortune. For instance, it was believed that wolf bones helped men to become strong and clever hunters. Some groups also wore jewelry—earrings, nose rings, and lip plugs—fashioned from ivory, shells, sandstone, or wood. Many men and women also sported tattoos as a form of decoration.

Arts and Crafts

The Inuit once made the tools, weapons, and other goods they needed to survive in the far north. With few trees in the Arctic, they had to use driftwood,

The Inuit carve sculptures to document key events. These sculptures come from the Northwest Territories Supreme Court.

stones, bones, and antlers. Sometimes, they traveled hundreds of miles to find suitable stones. They chipped the stones—flint, slate, and quartz—to make scrapers; points for arrows, harpoons, and spears; and knife blades, including the special curved blades for the knives known as **ulus**. Driftwood was made into tool and weapon handles as well as house and boat frames, boxes, and dishes. They fashioned various kinds of harpoons and spears known as atlatls. Men also skillfully wove nets and made snares for small animals. Caribou sinew was used as thread and fishing line. They shaped bones and antlers into weapons, notably harpoons and bows and arrows, and many tools, including knives, axes, scrapers, drills, thimbles, and needles. In their daily tasks, women relied most heavily on needles made of bone or ivory, sinew-backed knives, and chipped stone scrapers.

Men built light yet sturdy kayaks and umiaks for paddling over the icy waters. To make these boats they laid out a wooden frame lashed together with sinew. They sheathed the frame with sewn caribou or sealskins. A hole was left in the top of the kayaks for the propeller. Kayaks were propelled with a paddle with a blade on each end. Men used kayaks mainly for hunting. Because of their slender, graceful design, kayaks could be paddled swiftly and silently and were easily maneuvered in the water. Umiaks were large, open boats used for transportation and whaling. Men also made sleds pulled by hardy northern dogs known as huskies for travel during the winter. They lashed the wood frame together with strips of rawhide and made runners of wood or bone. They coated the runners with moss and ice so the dogsled would glide smoothly over the snow.

The Inuit were not only skilled craftspeople, but they were also talented artists. They expressed themselves through a variety of arts, from sculpture to singing. The arts were viewed as a means of achieving inner joy. Many Inuit carved pieces of bone, antler, or ivory into imaginative figurines, amulets, toys, and other small objects. Some groups also carved and painted wooden masks for dances and other ceremonies. Women artfully sewed furs into clothing not only for warmth but also as decorations on the garment. These objects were never intended to be exhibited—they were part of the everyday life and special ceremonies of the Inuit.

The Inuit were also known for their singing. People sang as they worked and as they played games. They sang as they danced or told stories. They sang to make fun of each other and to soothe frightened children. They sang about love and revenge, as well as hunting and animals. Songs were performed in a deep, nasal voice, which is sometimes called **throat singing**. People gathered in their igloos and rejoiced through songs when they had enough food. They also sang during the lean days of the bleakest winter as in this song:

> *Hard times, dearth times*
> *Plague us every one.*
> *Stomachs are shrunken,*
> *Dishes are empty*
> *Ayaa, yaa, yapape!*
> *Ayaa, yaa, yapape!*

Some songs were rooted in the Inuit's ancient origins, while others were composed spontaneously for feasts and festivals. Songs could belong to a person, family, or community. Whatever their nature, songs were heard everywhere, especially at dances. Among the Inuit who lived in the east, one man stood in the middle of the room and sang while in a state of ecstasy he danced and beat a drum. When he became exhausted, he passed the instrument to the next man and the dance continued.

Among the Inuit in the west, people often danced in groups. These dances varied in complexity among the people of Alaska and other regions. Dances included those with choreographed movements and those with no set movements. There were also sitting and kneeling dances in which people moved only their arms and heads.

They danced to entertain themselves and to illustrate stories. Dance was also a feature of special ceremonies such as the Wolf Dance. The Wolf Dance had several formal parts in which women and men faced each other. The women held wands adorned with feathers, and men wore headdresses of loon skin and long mittens.

Fun and Play

The Inuit enjoyed many games. In the hopping game, girls and boys competed to see who could hop on one foot the longest. During the brief warmth of summer, three or four people used an animal skin as a trampoline. As they jumped up and down, children learned to do tricks in the air. Children also played raven, a game similar to tag. One child, flapping his or her arms and cawing like a raven, hunted the others. The one who was caught became the next hunter. During the winter, adults played this game mainly to keep warm. Children liked a kind of hide-and-seek in which half of them formed a circle. They covered their eyes or looked at the ground while the others ran and hid. These children signaled when they were all hidden and those in the circle then looked for them. Children also played a game in which they threw spears at a willow hoop rolled on the ground or tossed in the air.

Adults played many games as well, including one similar to soccer. In this game, two teams kicked a ball covered with caribou skin, competing to see which team could keep possession of it. In *ajagak*, a cup-and-pin game, people swung a pin made of seal bone on a string. They tried to make the pin stick in each of ten holes (one for each of their fingers) drilled in a row in

The People and Culture of the Inuit

a large bone. The bone was tied to the other end of the string. They kept count by calling out, "Thumb, one finger, two finger …" In a similar game known as **nuglagaqtuq**, a bone with a hole was hung from a string. People tried to thrust a stick in the hole as the bone swung back and forth. The Inuit most often played games when they had gathered together during the long winter months. Other activities, such as cat's cradle, were enjoyed throughout the year. Inuit people made string figures. The figures known as "the two brown bears" and "man carrying a kayak" were popular throughout the Arctic.

Through all of these activities, men, women, and children joined together to become a community. Daily life was mostly difficult, and it took time to adapt to the harsh conditions of the Arctic, but once they did, the Inuit were able to enjoy games and other pastimes. Over the centuries, especially with the arrival of Europeans, Inuit communities became less nomadic and more permanent, entering a new era of Inuit history.

This photo shows the Inuit village of Kangaamiut, in western Greenland.

CHAPTER FOUR

We live on a diet of souls.

—Inuit shaman

BELIEFS OF THE INUIT

The Inuit, like other Native American groups, developed strong beliefs, practices, and traditions. These beliefs were honored and maintained over the centuries. Today, these beliefs have changed slightly but still hold a place in Inuit life.

The Living Earth

The Inuit believed that all things, living and nonliving, had souls. They sought to have a

This is an owl mask, one of many masks used in Inuit rituals and celebrations.

respectful relationship with these souls or spirits, especially those of game animals. This was thought to be necessary if people were to maintain health and well-being because a mistreated animal spirit could become a vengeful monster. People wore sacred amulets and called upon helpful spirits to protect them against evil spirits. Anyone who had suffered misfortune might wander away from the camp for several days and pray to the good spirits for help. The Inuit faced danger not only from the natural world, but from the spirit

The People and Culture of the Inuit

world as well. As one shaman explained, "We live on a diet of souls."

While the Inuit believed that everything had souls, they also believed that nature had a special impact on their everyday life. Sedna, the goddess of the sea, had a particular influence on Inuit religion and belief. The Inuit believed that as long as the sea was kept happy, they would always have food to eat. Other natural elements, such as the sun and the moon, also featured as part of their religious influences.

The environment also shaped many Inuit practices. They were strictly forbidden to hunt land and sea animals with the same weapons. They also carefully separated food and materials taken from the animals of each realm. Caribou meat had to be cooked on land and sealskins had to be sewn on the **sea ice**. Meat from sea and land animals could not be stored or cooked together. Caribou meat and freshwater fish, which were considered land creatures, could not be cooked when the Inuit were living on the sea ice, although they could be eaten raw. They could only be cooked on land but not over a fire made from driftwood, which comes from the sea.

The Inuit revered the polar bear because it inhabits both land and water. Because seals and other sea mammals lived in salt water, the Inuit believed that they were always thirsty, so their spirits were soothed if offered a drink of freshwater. It was believed that birds longed for oil, so the Inuit rubbed it on their heads, feet, and wing joints before plucking or skinning them. Spirits of the caribou were deeply offended if Inuit dogs were allowed to gnaw their bones near the

Polar bears are among the animals that share the Arctic with the Inuit.

place of their death. Wolves and bears were especially dangerous animals and, after a kill, the Inuit made special offerings—a little bow as a gift for a male animal and a strip of hide for a female. It was believed that, like humans, these animals would need these objects for hunting and sewing in the afterlife.

On the day after a kill, the Inuit did not sew out of respect for the animal. When a boy killed his first caribou or seal, his mother wept and ritually wrestled with him over the animal to give the impression that she respectfully mourned its death. The Inuit never mocked game animals or delighted in their pain for fear of being cursed. If they did not observe the proper rituals, the spirits of the air and the sky would be offended. Even the Mother of Sea Mammals, the most powerful spirit, might grow angry and punish them with starvation. The Inuit believed that showing delight during prosperous times might bring ill fortune, so they tended to be very modest and even complained about their good luck.

Healing and Rituals

People were also respectful of names. When a person died, everyone was forbidden to mention his or her name until a baby received the same name and brought the name back to life. It was believed that the

baby would inherit the good traits of the deceased. Similarly, it was considered bad luck to say one's name out loud. Upon arriving at another person's home, visitors simply announced themselves by saying, "Someone is here."

It was believed that both male and female shamans were in touch with the supernatural world and able to influence

An Inuit shaman sings while playing the drums in Thule, Greenland, circa 1906.

spirits. An individual underwent years of training before being considered a shaman, or angakok. Shamans attempted to cure sick people. When a person became seriously ill, the shaman was asked for assistance. The shaman entered into a trance to find the source of the difficulty and the appropriate treatment. By singing, dancing, and beating drums, he or she sought to communicate with the spirits. Occasionally, the spirits appeared to enter the shaman's body, who often rolled on the floor and spoke a strange language. The sick person was comforted that the shaman had at least acted on his or her behalf. Shamans watched over the health of the entire community. When a tragedy befell the group, they tried to ascertain who among them had broken a taboo. Shamans also served as leaders of the community. However, they were feared as much as they were honored. People believed that shamans had so much spiritual p they could harm anyone who offended them.

In sacred rituals, the Inuit appealed to varic elements of nature for good weather and succ hunting. Occasionally, they carved revered ob of wood, bone, and ivory, and decorated then fur or feathers. They also carved wooden mask resembled many animals and other spirits in n During dances, the men wore masks on their f the women placed miniature masks on their fir

This mask represents an Inuit shaman's spirit. It was believed a shaman could separate his spirit from his body and fly in spirit form to other parts of the world, where he would speak with other spirits.

Every year, the Inuit had two ceremonies during which they offered thanks for the elements that had helped them to survive. In the Bladder Festival, they sought to liberate the spirits of the whales that had been killed over the past year. Believing the spirits dwelled in the whale bladders, they inflated them with air. After several days of dancing and rituals, they returned the bladders

The landscape of Inuit territories is rocky and full of ice and snow.

to the sea. The second ceremony was held in the spring. After months of darkness, they dressed in attire that represented both male and female to symbolize creation and welcomed the return of the sun.

Telling Stories

Especially during the long, dark winters, the Inuit enjoyed dazzling stories about the sun, the moon, and the seas. These stories were often accompanied by songs, or the storyteller illustrated the tale by drawing pictures in the snow. Many stories dealt with the tension between contrasting but closely related elements—man and woman, land and sea, winter and summer, and dark and light. People not only enjoyed but learned about their way of life through these stories. Among many Inuit, music and storytelling are revered as the highest forms of art.

Stories often concerned survival. The Inuit have kept many of these stories alive by encouraging elders to retell them in schools and even on radio and television programs. Others are writing down the stories so they may not be lost to future generations.

Here is a story from Greenland about the little people who sometimes helped the Inuit survive the severe climate of their homeland:

There was once an old couple that had a daughter, and in the village where they lived there were many men who wanted to marry her. The parents, however, wished otherwise and made every effort to keep their daughter at home.

One man in particular was especially eager to make her his wife. He came repeatedly to the house, and at last he fought with the old father and nearly overpowered him. Running swiftly, the old man got to his boat, managed to load it, and narrowly escaped with his wife, daughter, and their belongings.

As they were pulling away, the rejected man and all the other men of the village shouted after them contemptuously, "It won't be easy now for you to get a husband for your daughter. The poor thing can't hunt. How dare you reject us. Just wait until you're hungry, then see if there's anyone to help you."

But the old man kept paddling without bothering to answer, and after a while the family landed on one of the outermost islands. There they built a new house and settled in for the winter.

One morning the old man awoke, saying, "What have I just seen? Was that a man gliding through the doorway?" He questioned his daughter, and as she kept silent he grew suspicious.

When he awoke the next morning he saw the same thing more clearly, a small, stout man slipping out the door. On being questioned, the daughter confessed, "Yes. I am married to one of the little people."

Upon hearing this news, the father did not get upset. His daughter continued, "My husband is afraid you won't like him, so he keeps out of sight. But if you do not mind, he will come live with us."

The next morning, when he opened his eyes, the old man turned toward the entrance and saw nothing unusual. Then, turning around to his daughter's resting place, he saw the little man sitting beneath her lamp.

The father was well pleased and leaned back on his sleeping platform, but when he looked over again, the little man was no longer there.

Toward evening the daughter left the house. When she returned, she had a hunting line, which she hung on a nail to dry. She turned to her parents and told them her husband had come back from hunting and had brought his catch, but now he had gone to take meat to his relatives.

Rushing outside to have a look, the old parents found many freshly killed seals on the beach and rejoiced to see that they were suddenly well supplied with food.

The following morning the old man peeped over the screen that separated him from his daughter's bed, and there was the son-in-law, seated beneath the lamp as before. In a little while the old man heard someone stirring, and by the time he got up, the son-in-law had already left.

The old man said to his daughter, "Why don't you tell him to spend time with us? We like him very much."

In the evening, when the little man returned with his catch, he stepped inside and made himself at home. The parents were thrilled to have him as a son-in-law, and the family lived happily through the rest of the winter.

When spring came, the son-in-law announced that they would soon be traveling to new hunting grounds for caribou. But first, he said, he would have to visit his own parents. Since he was their only son, he had to provide for them and for his sisters, too. So he went to see his family, and when he returned, it was time to start toward the caribou grounds.

The old father put everything into the boat, and when it was loaded and they were ready to set off, another boat suddenly appeared. It was the little man's relatives, come to guide them.

The two boats floated side by side and landed together that evening. The next morning they started out again. When they came in sight of an unfriendly village, the boat full of little people pulled out in front, and their headman called back to the other boat, "Keep close!" All of a sudden the two boats dived down and were paddling beneath the waves. Once past the unfriendly village, they rose back to the surface and safely continued on their way.

Reaching their destination, they made camp for the summer, and the little son-in-law went caribou hunting. When it was time to leave, they piled the boat high with furs and meat. The son-in-law had provided for them plentifully, and on returning to their winter quarters they were comfortable and well off.

Then, news came that the men who had once scorned the old father and his family were now at the point of starvation. Immediately the father set off for the mainland, and before long he returned with all the men who at one time had wished to marry his daughter. They came in a long train of kayaks. When they landed, they were treated hospitably, and the little son-in-law and his wife served them caribou and seal meat.

When the dishes had been set before the guests, the old man said to them in a loud voice, "I wonder if you can still remember what you were telling me a long time ago, when

As more Europeans arrived in Inuit communities, they converted some to Christianity. Here is an Inuit church.

you had nearly killed me, trying to steal my daughter. Can you remember? Your words were these: 'You will surely never get a clever son-in-law.' But in spite of your insults you see what I have. And you said you would never help me if I came to you hungry. Now, please, help yourselves, and eat as much as you like."

The People and Culture of the Inuit

Today practices such as storytelling remain an essential part of Inuit life. However, over time their religious beliefs have been mostly resigned to history. This had largely to do with the arrival of Europeans in the 1500s. Fur traders and missionaries coming to this newly explored region of the world mocked Inuit beliefs and refused to practice them when they came to the Arctic. The Inuit observed that the spirits did not avenge these offenses and began to doubt their own beliefs. As a result, many people abandoned their traditional religion and became Christians. In some cases, the respect for nature was also weakened. People came to believe that wildlife should be dominated and exploited by people, even if the environment was harmed in the process.

Today, many people continue to practice Christianity but also acknowledge and appreciate their Inuit ancestry and customs, and the environment has once again become a concern to the Inuit. Oil drilling and pollution are major issues the people of the Arctic are trying to combat. Climate change likewise worries them. It seems that after the arrival of Europeans and the introduction of a more Western way of living, the Inuit culture changed in ways they could never have imagined.

Sir Martin Frobisher

CHAPTER FIVE

We used to stay in igloos ... these days we mostly stay in tents.

—Inuk elder from Pangnirtung, Baffin Island, Canada

OVERCOMING HARDSHIPS

The Inuit spent many years developing their communities and living in the Arctic. Eventually, however, their world changed, particularly after the sixteenth century, with the steady stream of Europeans arriving. These newcomers—mostly men—sought to explore and settle the area.

In most cases, the Inuit were one of the last Native peoples to encounter Europeans. This was largely due to the climate in which they lived. However, in Greenland, the Inuit were actually one of the first peoples to meet Europeans. As early as 984 CE, the Greenland Inuit may have met a group of Vikings led by Erik the Red. However, another six centuries passed before Martin Frobisher, an English explorer, encountered the Inuit of Greenland and northern Canada in 1576. Frobisher and his party were searching for a water route known as the Northwest Passage, thought to join the Atlantic and Pacific Oceans. Landing on Baffin Island, Nunavut, Frobisher and his crew traded with the Inuit. However, not all of their interactions were peaceful. Before coming back to England, the English kidnapped an Inuit man and took him back to their native country. Frobisher later returned to the Arctic and captured three more Inuit—a man, a woman, and a child—and brought them to England. Sadly, all the captives died soon after they arrived. Over the years, as Europeans continued to search for the Northwest Passage, they traded metal knives, tools, and guns with the Inuit for fresh meat and fur clothes. The Inuit also acquired goods from the many ships wrecked on the ice.

A Changing World

In 1741, Vitus Bering, a Dane who explored for Russia and for whom the Bering Strait is named, became the first European to encounter the Inuit of Alaska. The region was soon after visited by Russian fur traders. In the late 1700s, Samuel Hearne, who worked for the Hudson's Bay Company, had made contact with the Inuit of northern Canada. The **niovayit**, or traders, supplied Inuit men with steel traps, guns, and ammunition in exchange for a wide variety of hides and furs. In Greenland, the Inuit heaped caribou, polar bear, seal, fox, and hare skins on dogsleds and hauled them

The Inuit use dogs and sleds to navigate the Arctic terrain.

to the trading post. In Canada, they trapped beavers, muskrats, minks, foxes, wolves, bears, and many other fur-bearing animals sought by the traders. In Alaska, men most often caught seals, beavers, muskrats, minks, and foxes, which they traded for sugar, coffee, tea, matches, and other goods.

By the early 1800s, many of the Inuit had begun to abandon their traditional way of life and had become dependent on European goods. They especially sought metal knives and kettles, guns, cloth, and lamps from the Russian, American, and Canadian traders, even though they were often cheated in the exchange. Alcohol was introduced to the Inuit, and it soon had a devastating effect on them.

When the United States acquired Alaska from Russia in 1867, the Americans embarked on many economic ventures, including fur trapping, gold mining, and whaling, that brought them into contact with the Inuit. Despite the flood of settlers, many Inuit groups managed to remain completely isolated from people of European descent until the early 1900s. However, they could not prevent changes from happening.

By 1900, the population of the Inuit had been devastated, due largely to the introduction of diseases for which the Inuit had no immunity. Things worsened for some Arctic communities in the 1950s when the Canadian government relocated peoples living in the High Arctic. These men, women, and children were promised plentiful land and food, and that they could return to their homelands in two years if they were unhappy. Despite this information, the areas the Inuit moved to did not have abundant resources and therefore many people suffered. This period was called the High Arctic Exile and remains a sore point in Inuit history.

Despite losing large numbers of people during the 1800s and 1900s, the Inuit persisted. The twentieth century became a time when more explorers tried to tackle land that had once only been traveled by the Inuit. The remaining Inuit became instrumental in helping these explorers. For example, they helped Admiral Robert E. Peary of the United States in his quest to become the first man to reach the North Pole. On April 6, 1909, Peary planted an American flag in the snow at the "Top of the World." Prior to making his famous journey, Peary had studied the Inuit language, habits, and style of dress. He not only won their trust and confidence but also learned to build snow houses and caches for storing food and to drive dog sleds. Four Inuit men—Ootah, Seegloo, Egingwah, and Ooqueah—and

Robert Peary poses in the Arctic with sled dogs.

Peary's partner Matthew Henson made the journey. He later said that he never would have reached the North Pole without the assistance of the Inuit.

The Language of the Inuit

Although scattered over thousands of miles of barren tundra and icy coastline, the Inuit all speak similar languages grouped by linguists as Eskimoan. Eskimoan and Aleut, the language of the Aleutian Islands of southwestern Alaska, form the Eskimo-Aleut family. This language family may be distantly related to the Ural-Altaic languages spoken in Finland, Hungary, and Turkey.

Life for the Inuit may be difficult, but they also manage to have a sense of humor.

The People and Culture of the Inuit

The Inuit have numerous words for snow, ice, wind, and other features of their environment. The language has also contributed many words to the English language, such as parka, igloo, kayak, husky, and malamute. The following examples are based on an English-Eskimo dictionary compiled by Arthur Thibert and published in Canada. Most letters are pronounced as in English, with the following exceptions:

k	as in *k*ing, but occasionally pronounced deep in the throat like *kr* without the *r* being distinctly rolled or spoken. This *k* is noted as *kr* when the alternate pronunciation is required.
j	as *y* in *y*ou
y	as *y* in *y*ou
s	as in *s*hip, although some groups pronounce it as *h* (for example, *asso*, meaning "enough," is pronounced *aho*)
i	as in k*ee*n
u	as in sh*oo*t
ng	as in si*ng*ing, never as o*ng*oing
dlerk	at the end of a sentence is pronounced *tslerk*. Along with *kr*, it is the only really difficult pronunciation.

innark, aktok	adult
nagdjuk	antler
nutaralak	baby
iglerk	bed
paunrait	berries
tingmiark	bird
orkso	blubber
tuktu	caribou
nutara, soruserk, krittongak, piarak	child
igalerk	chimney
koliktar	coat
nigliktok	cold
panik	daughter
ublarpaluk	dawn
kraumayok	daylight
kringmerk	dog
tibjak	driftwood
krilaut	drum
mannik	egg
ikkuma	fire
irkaluk	fish
natterk	floor
nipterk, tarkserk	fog
nerkriksak	food
patu	frost
koak	frozen meat

amerk mitkrolik	fur
niviasar	girl, young
adgauyait, poalu	gloves
erngutak, ernrutak	grandchild
tuyurmiangoyok	guest
krauyimatauyok	guide
nauligak, unark, kapût	harpoon (spear)
aisimabvik, ainiarvik	home
iglu	house
ui	husband
sikku, koasak	ice
pikaluyak	iceberg
kekertak	island
nuna	land, earth
inuk	man
nulliarengnerk	marriage
nerkri	meat
immiugak	melting ice (for water)
unnuar kretirarlugo	midnight
poalu	mitten
tatkret	moon
tatkresiwok	moon, full
ublar	morning
manerk	moss
unnuar	night
kannernark	north

nanuk	polar bear
tareor	sea
netjerk, netserk	seal
krilak	sky
kamotik, kramotik	sled
apingaut	snow (first snowfall)
ernerk	son
ublureak	star
auyark, auyak	summer
sikrinerk	sun
ajokertuye, illiniartitsiye	teacher
iglurdjuartalik	village
aiverk	walrus
immerk	water
sila	weather
orksok	whale blubber
nilliak	wife
arnak	woman

A New Age

As years passed and areas of Inuit land became more populated by European and American settlers, the Inuit way of life also began to change. Rather than maintaining certain traditions, they started to adapt to Western lifestyles and trends. For example, in the nineteenth century, many men, women, and children began wearing European- and American-style clothes. They also stopped traveling for different seasons and established permanent communities. The structures of

The People and Culture of the Inuit

Many Inuit communities are gaining more access to technology and influences of the Western world.

their housing also changed over time, influenced by the houses Europeans and Americans built. Today, the Inuit continue to uphold their culture and practices, but it is becoming increasingly difficult for communities to live a solely Inuit lifestyle. With the advent of the Internet and social media, more Inuit are becoming connected to Western traditions and behaviors. It is a worry that Inuit traditions may fade from memory as more young people rely on Western technologies.

An Inuit girl holds up an Aleut mask.

A piece of paper from
the outside world is as
thin as the shell of a
snowbird's egg.

—Kenojuak Ashevak,
Inuit artist

THE NATION'S PRESENCE NOW

Since the introduction of European and
American lifestyles, the Inuit way of life has
not been the same. Many modern Inuit
communities have adopted Western cultural
practices, such as technology, social media,
and ways of speaking. Some elders today
believe younger generations risk forgetting the
Inuit traditions altogether. They are working
to preserve their culture in ways that speak to

people of the twenty-first century. It is their hope that the Inuit beliefs and practices will continue to be celebrated for many generations to come.

The Inuit Today

Over the course of the twentieth and twenty-first centuries, the Inuit population has climbed, with more than 135,000 Native people living in the sprawling territory today, yet many modern advances— manmade and environmental— threaten Inuit culture and tradition. Oil drilling, mining, and large-scale commercial fishing and whaling, along with issues of global warming, have drastically reduced the populations of land and sea animals. This in turn has forced the Inuit to adopt different ways of survival. No longer able to enjoy plentiful amounts of important foods, they must find other ways to feed and provide for themselves.

The Inuit community has changed over time. Most Inuit communities are small, with populations ranging from 500 to 6,700. The largest Inuit community in Canada is Iqaluit, the capital of Nunavut, with 6,699 people as of 2011. Each village has stores, one or two schools, and an airport. They have a few

Many Inuit families have built houses and live a more modern lifestyle.

roads around their villages, where people can drive; however, many communities depend on scheduled flights from their local airport to get around. Airplanes are also used to deliver food and other supplies. Many Inuit have adopted European tools, including metal guns and knives, sewing machines, snowmobiles, and motorboats. Many people have moved into permanent wood-frame houses, which has made their old ways of seasonal migration seem impractical and out-of-date.

The Inuit get many commodities and supplies delivered to them by plane.

Some of these homes have septic and water tanks, while others do not have running water. Many people rely on a water truck that brings water to them.

In recent years, many Inuit have continued to adopt a more modern way of life, including the use of computers and other technology. More and more young people are connected to social media, such as Facebook, Instagram, Twitter, and Snapchat. These outlets provide

The People and Culture of the Inuit

ways for the Inuit to connect to one another but also ways in which they can perhaps forget their Inuit roots and become engrossed in other Western traditions. Many Inuit live as other North Americans, taking jobs, shopping at supermarkets, and enjoying life inside a home. The Inuit in Greenland have been especially influenced by Danish culture, while the people of Siberia have been affected by the political changes of the former Soviet Union and now Russia. Instead of families providing for themselves, many Inuit in Siberia now hunt seals, walruses, and whales as part of a group known as a collective. In other regions, some Inuit groups have begun to herd reindeer or cattle and grow crops hardy enough to survive the brief, chilly summers.

In Alaska, the Inuit remained isolated until the mid-1900s when the US government began to provide them with basic schools and medical services. The discovery of gas and oil, as well as the surge in mining operations, also brought dramatic changes. American workers poured into the region, and many Inuit took jobs on the construction projects. Similarly, because of oil and mineral exploitation, the Inuit of Canada have also come into much greater contact with the outside world in recent years. Many Alaska Inuit have left their small communities and moved to cities. Today, many live in urban areas, away from their friends and families.

In 1971, the Alaska Inuit received $962 million and 44 million acres (17.8 million hectares) of land in exchange for giving up their claim to 335 million acres (135.6 million ha). Known as the Alaska Native Claims Settlement Act (ANCSA), this agreement was reached largely because the United States government planned to permit construction of the Trans-Alaska Pipeline across Inuit territory. In this agreement, the Inuit and other Native peoples gained legal ownership of 12 percent of Alaska and received funds desperately needed for economic development. Many Inuit villages in Alaska have formed corporations to more effectively represent their interests. In 1980, the US government amended ANCSA with the Alaska National Interest Lands Conservation Act (ANILCA). This measure restored rights of Native peoples to hunt and fish their lands and water.

In Canada, the Inuit movement for self-determination began in the 1970s. In 1976, a Native organization called Inuit Tapirisat of Canada (today called the Inuit Tapiriit Kantami, or ITK) put forth a proposal to form a new territory called Nunavut, which means "our land." In 1982, a vote was held on establishing the territory, to be created out of the eastern and northern parts of the Northwest Territories. Over 80 percent of the Inuit population—

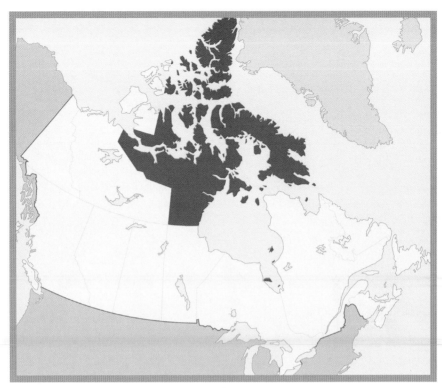

Canada is a vast country. The area in red is Nunavut.

and 56 percent of the Northwest Territories' total population—approved the proposal. In 1993, the Canadian Parliament passed two new laws, the Nunavut Act and the Nunavut Land Claims Agreement Act. The first officially established Nunavut as a territory—it would take effect in 1999, after a transitional period. The second, the largest land claim settlement in Canadian history, gave the Inuit complete control of about 135,000 square miles (350,000 sq km) of land, or roughly 20 percent of the new territory. The Inuit were also granted payment of $1.14 billion over the course of fourteen years in exchange for relinquishing all other land claims in Canada. Today, Nunavut is home to over 36,000 residents, about 80 percent of whom are Inuit.

Many areas of the Arctic suffer effects from climate change.

Looking to the Future

The Inuit are struggling to maintain their traditional ways at the distant edges of a modern world. With less game and fish, along with limits on hunting endangered animals, people have greater difficulty providing for themselves. Likewise, global warming has affected the region. According to a 2015 article from *Slate*, "Alaska

is heating up at twice the rate of the rest of the country." Many Inuit and other residents of the area and elsewhere in the Arctic are finding it difficult to adapt to changing climate behavior. This means they must also change some of their traditions. They must now purchase much of their food and household goods. Yet transporting groceries and goods over long distances by plane, truck, or boat is expensive, so people must pay high prices. With few jobs in villages, many people leave their homes and families to work at seasonal jobs in mills, mines, or fish-processing plants. Many Inuit have sought employment with oil companies.

Many parents encourage their children to study hard in school and to attend college to become teachers, engineers, business managers, doctors, and lawyers. Although more schools are being constructed, many young people must still leave home to attend high school. They miss their families, yet many people believe that this is the only way they will have a chance for a prosperous life. Many Inuit also use the radio and the Internet to communicate among far-flung settlements, as well as for education and social services. At the same time, however, the Inuit do not wish their children to lose touch with their heritage. Older people often come to school to share traditional stories and show children how to sew and make fish traps. Men still teach their sons how to hunt seals and how to survive winter storms. They want their children

This is an image of the *Never Alone* video game, which is inspired by Inuit culture and folktales.

to know that they can make a living and love the land of their ancestors.

One specific way elders are trying to preserve Inuit history and stories in the minds of younger people today is through technology. In 2014, a group of Inuit called the Iñupiat, along with a children's educational game company called E-Line Media, created a video game based on the stories of Iñupiat ancestors. This game, called *Never Alone*, blends Iñupiat traditional storytelling with modern technology. In it, the main character, Nuna, and her pet fox tackle monsters

The People and Culture of the Inuit

and situations from Inuit folklore. This is a unique way that one Inuit community is embracing Western developments as a teaching tool. However, this step also has caused controversy. Regardless, it is a method for reminding Inuit children and young people of their ancestry, and the importance of keeping that ancestry alive in a quickly changing environment.

The Inuit today have many opportunities their ancestors did not. They live a more grounded lifestyle while working hard to keep their culture and practices going. They have opened museums, tourist companies, and education centers to keep their culture alive and in the minds of modern societies around the world. While many communities find a balance between Western influences and Inuit culture, the Inuit people must continue to work hard to preserve their history, culture, and traditions.

Kenojuak Ashevak,
circa 1997

CHAPTER SEVEN

Let us show you our world.

—Christian Eyfa, Greenland Inuit member and hunter

FACES OF THE INUIT NATION

Over the years, there have been many men and women who have influenced Inuit history. Through their accomplishments, they have remained a part of Inuit memory. Here are some of the most influential Inuit names in recent times.

Kenojuak Ashevak (1927–2013), artist, was born on Baffin Island, Northwest Territories, Canada (today part of Nunavut). The daughter of Ushuakjuk, a hunter and trader, and his wife Seelaki, Kenojuak was named after her deceased maternal grandfather. When her father was murdered in a dispute in their camp in 1933, Kenojuak went to live with her grandmother, Koweesa, who taught her sewing.

When Kenojuak was nineteen, her mother and stepfather, Takpaugni, arranged for her to marry a hunter named Johnniebo. A spirited young woman, she threw rocks at her husband, but came to love him as a kind and gentle man. In the early years of her marriage, she gave birth to two daughters who died of food poisoning and a son who was adopted by another family at birth. Adoption was a common Inuit custom. In 1950, the first nurse arrived in the north to offer medical care. Kenojuak was diagnosed with tuberculosis and sent to Parc Savard Hospital in Quebec City, where she was treated from 1952 to 1955. During this time, she made dolls and did beadwork.

When she returned to her family in the north, Kenojuak began to devote herself to her art, notably sealskin and beaded crafts. She also began carving and drawing. With the encouragement of James Houston, an early supporter of Inuit art, she persevered and in 1958 her first print, *Rabbit Eating Seaweed*, was made from a design on one of her sealskin bags. With Houston's help, Kenojuak and several other Inuit of Cape Dorset formed the West Baffin Eskimo Cooperative in 1959. The group served as a *senlavik*, or "place where one works." Several of Kenojuak's drawings were displayed and favorably reviewed. In 1962, the National Film Board of Canada made a documentary about her life entitled *Eskimo Artist—Kenojuak* that brought considerable public attention to her work.

In 1967, Kenojuak received the Order of Canada Medal of Service, and her work was featured in the National Gallery of Canada. She became especially well known for the vivid colors and intricate design of her drawings of birds and people. Three years later, one of her most famous works, *The Enchanted Owl*, appeared on a six-cent Canadian postage stamp. In 1972, she was honored with membership in the Royal Canadian Academy, and over the years her work was widely exhibited in Canada, the United States and Europe. In 1986, a thirty-year retrospective of her work was exhibited at the McMichael Canadian Collection Gallery in Kleinsburg, Ontario, just outside Toronto. Although she was best known for her drawings and paintings, she also carved and sculpted soapstone. She died in 2013 after battling cancer, but her works and achievements are forever remembered. In 2014, on what would have been her eighty-seventh birthday, Google recognized her accomplishments in a Google doodle drawing, uplifting her and celebrating all that she did during her lifetime.

Terry Audla (1970–), spokesperson, chairperson, and journalist, is the president of Inuit Tapiriit Kantami, the national representative body of over sixty thousand Inuit living around the world. He was born in Frobisher Bay, Northwest Territories (today known as Iqaluit, the capital of Nunavut), the son of Walter and Rynie Audla. He speaks for all Inuit members around North America

Terry Audla speaks during a news conference in 2012.

The People and Culture of the Inuit

and the rest of the world every year. He is an advocate for his people as well as for issues surrounding the Inuit, including the environment, education, and Native rights. He has contributed to periodicals such as the *Huffington Post*, discussing issues important to the livelihood of the Inuit people.

William L. Hensley (1941–), also known as Iggiagruk, which means "Big Hill" or "Little Mountain," has served as a Native leader in Alaska since he graduated from George Washington University in 1966. While studying in Washington, DC, he wondered why his people,

William Hensley, circa 2010

who lived in poverty, were not represented in Congress. He became one of the founders of the Alaska Federation of Natives (AFN), an organization that represents many villages and a number of social service organizations. With Hensley serving in several key positions, the AFN successfully lobbied Congress to pass the Alaska Native Claims Settlement Act of 1971, legislation that granted nearly

$1 billion and 44 million acres (17.8 million ha) of land to Alaskan Natives.

In 1968, Hensley was appointed to serve on the National Council on Indian Opportunity. He also received the John F. Kennedy Memorial Award, the National Public Service Award from the Rockefeller Foundation, and many other honors. He was elected to the Alaska House of Representatives for two terms, serving from 1967 to 1971 before serving as a state senator from 1970 to 1974. Hensley again served as senator in 1986. Over the years, he has remained active in public service, including programs in education, suicide prevention, and alcohol abuse. He has also been actively involved with wildlife management and the hunting and fishing rights of Alaskan Natives.

Rebecca Kudloo (ca. 1949–), Inuit spokesperson and advocate for women's rights, is the president of Pauktuutit, an organization that seeks to improve the lives and treatment of Inuit women in Canada and elsewhere. She has worked for over twenty-five years in counseling-based organizations and was elected president of Pauktuutit in 2013. Every year she speaks at many women's rights conferences and conventions throughout the world. She seeks to improve Inuit women and children's lives, to provide them with an outlet when needed, and to educate them in methods of self-defense if needed. She wishes to change the way women are viewed in Inuit society and around the world, and to provide Inuit women a safe space to discuss topics important to them.

Rebecca Kudloo is a women's rights advocate.

Howard Rock

Howard Rock (1911–1976), editor and publisher, was born in Point Hope, Alaska. As a young man, he attended St. Thomas Mission and later worked his way to the Pacific Northwest where he studied art at the University of Washington in Seattle. He became a jewelry designer. During World War II, he served in the US Army Air Force in North Africa. After the war, Rock returned to Alaska where he became active in public service. Recognizing the need for a Native newspaper, he sought financial support and established the *Tundra Times* in 1962. Serving as publisher and editor, he became highly regarded for his strong advocacy of the rights of Alaska Natives. A year before his death, he was nominated for a Pulitzer Prize.

The Inuit have had many important and influential members living among them. These men and women continue to influence Inuit history and remain important figures of hope and inspiration for Inuit members today.

CHRONOLOGY

Between 3000 and 1000 BCE Inuit migrate on foot and by dogsled from Siberia to North America across the Bering Strait long after other peoples had come to the continent. Some scholars believe the time of migration may have been earlier, between 6000 and 5000 BCE.

984 CE Led by Erik the Red, the Vikings reach Greenland and perhaps make contact with the Inuit.

1576 Martin Frobisher, an English explorer, encounters the Central Inuit of northern Canada.

1741 Vitus Bering, an explorer for Russia, is the first European to make contact with the Inuit of Alaska.

1867 The United States acquires Alaska from Russia.

1900 The Inuit population is devastated by diseases.

1909 With help of the Inuit, Admiral Robert E. Peary and Matthew Henson of the United States reach the North Pole on April 6.

1971 In the Alaska Native Claims Settlement Act (ANCSA), the Inuit of Alaska receive $962 million and

44 million acres (17.8 million ha) of land in exchange for giving up claims to 335 million acres (135.6 million ha).

1982 Residents of the Northwest Territories vote in favor of creating Nunavut, meaning "our land," out of the northern and eastern parts of the territory.

1993 Canadian Parliament passes the Nunavut Act, allowing for the creation of the new territory, and the Nunavut Land Claims Agreement Act, giving the Inuit control over about 20 percent of the territory and granting them payment of $1.14 billion over the next fourteen years.

1999 Nunavut officially becomes Canada's newest territory.

2010 The Inuit call this year the Year of the Inuit and throw celebrations all year long.

2011 The population of Iqaluit, Nunavut, reaches 6,699.

GLOSSARY

aglu A breathing hole in the ice used by seals.

amaut A parka hood in which a baby was kept warm.

amulet A small sacred object believed to provide protection and bring good fortune.

angakok A shaman with powers for healing the body and spirit.

barrens An extent of usually level land with little vegetation.

Bering Strait The body of water that separates Russia and Alaska. During the last Ice Age, a land bridge across the strait allowed for migration from one continent to the other.

blubber Fat from a whale or other sea mammal, often melted and eaten as food or used as oil for lamps.

cache A hiding place for food and belongings. Also the act of storing items in such a hiding place.

igloo An Inuit house made of snow, skin, or other materials.

infanticide The practice of intentionally allowing a baby to die.

inua A spirit or soul, especially of a game animal.

kamiks Insulated shoes made of animal skins; also called mukluks.

karmat A square or rectangular house built by Inuit, especially by those living in Greenland and Alaska.

kashim A large building used by men for ceremonies.

kayak A slender, pointed canoe sheathed with animal skins, with a hole on top in which the paddler sits.

kudlik A lamp used to warm a home and dry clothing.

mukluks Warm shoes made of animal skins; also called kamiks.

muktuk The layer of fat under a whale's skin.

niovayit A trader.

nuglagaqtuq A popular Inuit game.

sea ice Ice that forms on the ocean as a solid sheet or as ice floes.

sinew Tough animal tissue joining muscle to bone and used by the Inuit as thread.

spawning Laying eggs.

taboo A required or forbidden practice that ensures health and well-being.

throat singing A type of singing within the throat that makes a deep, nasal sound.

tundra Low, treeless land of the north that becomes marshy in the warm months but never thaws beneath the surface.

ulu A curved knife.

umiak An open boat covered in animal skins in which several people hunt or travel together.

weir A low wall or dam built across a stream or river.

BIBLIOGRAPHY

Anderson, Alun. *After the Ice: Life, Death, and Geopolitics in the New Arctic*. Washington, DC: Smithsonian, 2009.

Banerjee, Subhankar, ed. *Arctic Voices: Resistance at the Tipping Point*. New York: Seven Stories Press, 2013.

Christopher, Neil, ed. *Unikkaaqtuat: An Introduction to Inuit Myths and Legends*. Toronto, ON: Inhabit Media, 2011.

Cunningham, Kevin, and Peter Benoit. *The Inuit*. True Books: American History. New York: Scholastic, 2011.

Dorais, Louis-Jacques. *The Language of the Inuit: Syntax, Semantics, and Society in the Arctic*. Montreal, QC: McGill-Queen's University Press, 2010.

Emmerson, Charles. *The Future History of the Arctic*. New York: PublicAffairs, 2010.

Evyagotailak, Darla, and Mindy Willett. *No Borders: Kigliqangittuq*. The Land Is Our Storybook. Markham, ON: Fifth House Publishers, 2013.

Falconer, Shelley, and Shawna White. *Stones, Bones and Stitches: Storytelling Through Inuit Art*. Lord Museum. Toronto, ON: Tundra Books, 2007.

Ipellie, Alootook, and David MacDonald. *The Inuit Thought of It: Amazing Arctic Inventions*. We Thought of It. Richmond Hill, ON: Annick Press, 2007.

Krupnik, Igor, Shari Gearhead, Claudio Aporta, Lene Kielsen Holm, and Gita J. Laidler, eds. *SIKU: Knowing Out Ice: Documenting Inuit Sea-Ice Knowledge and Use*. London: Springer, 2010.

McGrath, Melanie. *The Long Exile: A Tale of Inuit Betrayal and Survival in the High Arctic*. New York: Vintage, 2008.

McGregor, Heather E. *Inuit Education and Schools in the Eastern Arctic*. Vancouver, BC: UBC Press, 2010.

Stern, Pamela. *Historical Dictionary of the Inuit*. 2nd ed. Historical Dictionaries of Peoples and Cultures. Lanham, MD: Scarecrow Press, 2013.

Wright, Shelley. *Our Ice Is Vanishing: A History of Inuit, Newcomers, and Climate Change*. Montreal, QC: McGill-Queen's University Press, 2014.

Zellen, Barry Scott. *On Thin Ice: The Inuit, the State, and the Challenge of Arctic Sovereignty*. Lanham, MD: Lexington Books, 2009.

FURTHER INFORMATION

Want to know more about the Inuit? Check out these websites, videos, and organizations.

Websites

Inuit Cultural Online Resource

icor.ottawainuitchildrens.com

This website provides detailed information about the Inuit way of life, their traditions, and history.

Never Alone: Could a Video Game Help to Preserve Inuit Culture?

www.newyorker.com/tech/elements/never-alone-video-game-help-preserve-inuit-culture

This *New Yorker* article describes the *Never Alone* video game project and how it preserves Inuit culture.

Videos

Inuit Throat-Singing Demonstration

www.youtube.com/watch?v=8IqOegVCNKI

This video demonstrates throat singing, an Inuit tradition.

Inuit Wisdom

video.nationalgeographic.com/video/exploreorg/inuit-wisdom-eorg

This video explores Inuit life and wisdom from the elders.

Life in Iqaluit, Nunavut

www.youtube.com/watch?v=x3olPvBuFA4

This video shows Iqaluit, Nunavut, in the winter and describes what it is like to live in the town.

On Thin Ice: Inuit Way of Life Vanishing in Arctic

www.youtube.com/watch?v=nTDNbaU33TA

This video features Inuit hunters in Greenland and examines how climate change is threatening their way of life.

Organizations

Inuit Circumpolar Council Canada

75 Albert Street Suite 1001
Ottawa, ON K1P 5E7
Canada
www.inuitcircumpolar.com
(613) 563-2642

Makkovik Inuit Community

16 Andersen Street
PO Box 132
Makkovik, NL A0P 1J0
Canada
www.makkovik.ca/home
(709) 923-2221

Museum of Inuit Art
207 Queen's Quay West
Toronto, ON M5J 1A7
Canada
www.miamuseum.ca
(416) 640-1571

Nunavut Tourism
PO Box 1450
Iqaluit, NU X0A 0H0
Canada
www.nunavuttourism.com
(866) 686-2888

INDEX

Page numbers in **boldface** are illustrations. Entries in **boldface** are glossary terms.

The People and Culture of the Inuit

The People and Culture of the Inuit

ABOUT THE AUTHOR

Raymond Bial has published more than eighty books—most of them photography books—during his career. His photo-essays for children include *Corn Belt Harvest, Amish Home, Frontier Home, Shaker Home, The Underground Railroad, Portrait of a Farm Family, With Needle and Thread: A Book About Quilts, Mist Over the Mountains: Appalachia and Its People, Cajun Home,* and *Where Lincoln Walked.*

As with his other work, Bial's deep feeling for his subjects is evident in both the text and illustrations. He travels to tribal cultural centers, photographing homes, artifacts, and surroundings and learning firsthand about the national lifeways of these peoples.

The emeritus director of a small college library in the Midwest, he lives with his wife and three children in Urbana, Illinois.